The Subject of:
Life Living Life Politics Love

DONALD D. CONLEY, SR.

ISBN: 978-1-6987-0635-1 (sc)
ISBN: 978-1-6987-0634-4 (e)

Trafford rev. 02/27/2021

 www.trafford.com
North America & international
toll-free: 844-688-6899 (USA & Canada)
fax: 812 355 4082

INTERPRETATIONS

On **Verity**: The Truth of Something
On **Supplication**: To ask humbly
On **Axiom**: An accepted general truth or principle

CONTENTS

ABOUT THE AUTHOR

After spending a good portion of my life in first California's State prison system for a series of armed robberies over a span of five years ultimately landing me in the Federal Prison system with a sentence of Thirty-Three years in 1978 I for one admit that if it were not for being sent to prison surely life would have been anything but normal and or possibly still in existence for me At the age of 70 life is no more a mystery but instead a canvas on which to paint making it out to be whatever you want for the world to see without any of the Regrets Reservations or Restrictions

Life is what it is and what ever "That" is it's up to you to make it happen

In Comparison

The nearest thing
To God I know
Here on earth
Is knowing Love

And loving you
Is showing me
Each day
Exactly what He does

No hidden dark agenda
With motives all unseen
A blessing in a precious gift
Not only found in dreams

Such beauty all around me
I had not realized before
Not until you took my hand that now
I live to love you more

Rhythm Of Life

Life itself is a Rhythm
With an origin too elaborate to equate
Like the reasons for a gentle breeze
Or the most violent of some earthquakes

People question how to go on living
When the life of a loved one is lost
The answer is simply One day at a time
For that same love we defer the cost

Pain exchanged in reproducing life
From pleasure sought one loving night
Must be endured for allowing love to run wild
Maybe even longer after birth of a child

To query explanation about Destiny
Forever remains a great mystery
The reason oceans ebb and flow
Are Rhythms of life that no one knows

PLAGUE OR PLIGHT

The root of all evil
This word adjectively exist
Centered in the Mother Land
Deep inside of it

Found miles below the ground
Upon which Free Men of color live
They embrace no other heritage
And accept none that outsiders try to give

Daily they are massacred
The indiscriminate wholesale killing
Their wives and children sold
Bought by Arabs who are most willing

Young girls of ten and twelve are raped
All by the Arabic of speech
While miles away over in this land
Other's profit from what they teach

"There but for the Grace of God go I"
Can easily all be said
But ask yourself if in their shoes
Would you be alive or dead

Events that plague modern man
Slavery still exist in the Sudan
China Russia and Libya to name three
All have a hand in this drudgery

Some scholars say this was meant to be
Each soul must fulfill its own destiny
For mastery all men can claim
To a level where it knows no shame
Though shocking as it is revealed
To whom or what is the appeal
What justifies the right or wrong
Look at how long this has gone on

Instill foreign will upon any man
One of two things he shall do the best that he can
One fight what he finds as a Tyranny
Or be what the Master wants him to be

Love

To enjoy enthusiastically
Joyfully and complete
Each time is as the first time
Found swept off my feet

Eagerly uninhibited
No inimical intentions
A luminous aura suddenly appears
The instant certain sounds are mentioned

Breathtaking to ones own minds eye
Such desire welled up inside
Imagining great ecstasy
At the pleasure from a single smile

Contained within four letters
Like a blessing from above
This special gift once it is found
Is something known as Love

INFLICTED ADDICTION
(PART ONE)

Horace got his brains blown out
Carlos died of A.I.D.S.
Both victims of Heroin
From which nothing else could save
Then came the Rock
Some called it Crack
The same type of drug
Only government backed
Designed to destroy
The free will and minds of many
Until what justice for all
There would not be any
Poison's both strategically placed
An attempt by some to control a race
A whole population meant to be tamed
It is common knowledge at who it is aimed

SUPPLICATION

FOR STRENGTH

Great Spirit look down on me
Behind these bars of steel
So far away from my homeland
To you Great Spirit I appeal
Now in this hour of darkness
In your wisdom show me light
So that I may stand in spite of this
Learning the ways of what is right
I ask you too Great Spirit
To protect and guide my soul
Watch over those and all I love
Their very lives in Your Hands You hold
Great Spirit grant me wisdom
Let me drink as if from a well
So that I may share with my Brotherhood
Only goodness that you compel

For Strength

My hope and faith everlasting
That You will keep me strong
Knowing you are there to guide me
And I will soon be home

I wrote this piece for Dallas Thunder-Shield who was 21 at the time when he was shot and killed attempting to escape from federal prison with Lenard Peltier His contribution to the Wounded Knee Movement. Two week after I wrote this it turned out to be his epitaph

LOVING YOU

I've always wanted
To do so many things
In my life before
I leave this earth
Write the greatest
All American Novel
Travel across the
Country with no...
Particular destination
Other than just going
To be going...
I have always wanted
To know happiness
Peace of mind far
And above anything else

Con't.

Loving You

More than any...
Acquisition destination
Place or thing...
The most wonderful
Experience of my life
Has been loving you

BITTERSWEET

I knew the taste of honey
A flavor from your kiss
Then learned the pain of sorrow
How love could be like this

The first time my eyes held you
All of life seemed to stand still
An event I cannot soon forget
Or believe I ever will

From start there was this pleasure
Too enormous to explain
But in one instant flash of light
It all turned into pain

Con't.

Bittersweet

Yet still I seek that aura
Of what brought me such delight
Though well aware of consequences
I am compelled to take this flight

IRRESISTIBLE

In my mind's eye
I was swept up in a dream
Dancing among the stars
As the moon began to sing

Occurring at the break of day
Staying with me all the while
Then every time I thought of you
To my face it brought a smile

I could feel your soft caresses
So exciting against my skin
But once I saw the morning light
I wanted to feel it again

Con't.

Irresistible

The trouble with a fantasy
Especially one so real
Is how a little taste of Heaven
Becomes irresistible to steal

A Gift Of Time

So close we are together
Even when far apart
Time or distance has no voice
Within our fledging hearts

A love forever youthful
Given new birth every day
Enveloped in a pulchritude
Of your sweet and loving ways

Gifts that are worth giving
Need not come from another heart
With yourself is the beginning
The first place you should start

Con't.

Gift of Time

A sumptuous endowment
Priceless beyond reach
Yes is contained within your grasp
You need only stop and seek

AXIOM

I Understand

Everything must change
It is a basic part of life
What thrives throughout the day
May cease to exist at night

Life right at its longest
Can prove to be very short
Like what is accepted as truth today
Tomorrow will be easy to distort

I understand the changes
Those constant ups and downs
Realizing too that on my turn
I will no longer be around

Con't

I understand

Understand beyond the shadow
Please let there be no doubt
That all my love and sympathy
Right now to you goes out

REMEMBERING

Remembering the first time
Riding on two wheels
Starting out a little nervous
Until confidence finds the feel

That initial test in water
Somewhat harrowing and deep
Reflecting on a nightmare once
About drowning in my sleep

Evaluation in education
Although thought of as tuff
A process all so constant
One cannot seem to get enough

Con't.

Remembering

But of every life taught lesson
To revere right from the start
Is the one obtained from The Energy
The real source of your beating heart

I Choose To Be With You

Who else would know my story
As well as you do
And who else could I trust to tell
All my troubles to

There's not one soul
With whom I feel
Knows me better than you do
Nor is there one single heart
With a love so sweet and true

That's why I choose to be with you
To last my whole life through
Today for now for ever
I choose to be with you

Con't.

My life has had its share
Of ups and downs
Throughout the bad and good
You have always been around

You help provide the reason
To what I'm living for
Just when I think there's nothing left
You begin to show me more

Therefore I choose to be with you
To last my whole life through
Today for now for ever
I choose to be with you

We started out as simply friends
Like two ships sailing in the night
Each watch for the other
Not ever losing sight

SEARCHING

Why is love so hard to find?
Because it's more than just a state of mind
Involving the soul and body too
Along with someone else who feels like you

How can you be really sure
That once it's found it will endure
Not a game of chance at best I say
Since people find it every day

Remember what you give away
It is precisely what you keep
Therefore do take heed
To exactly what you seek

Con't

Searching

Your true nature will be the catalyst
Giving you what you attract
But once it is acquired
You cannot give it back

Space and Time is impossible to erase
No matter how desperately you wail your case
There are no judges or Powers that Be
Only your own mind can set you free

No Paradise

Socrates was put to death
For teaching people to think for themselves
While Jesus too was crucified
And those who followed him put in prison cells

If it is true that man cannot govern himself
How is it that another man can rule the other
Since he is the one who makes the rules
But does not treat him as a loving brother

Politics and corporate tricks
Have no place for human feelings
The reality of this fact
Can send the faint of heart to reeling

Con't

No Paradise

Paradise simply put
can easily be found
It is not a person place or thing
Even found from within the ground

There is no such thing as paradise
At least not on this earth
Since in the end when all is said and done
We each will turn to dirt

Yet the earth may bare its own wicked fruit
Bitter and foul to the taste
But in your own mind you have the ability
For your own paradise you can create

UBIQUITOUS

I want to make love to you
My dearest precious Sweet
Tasting you from the top of your head
Down to the bottom of your pretty feet

I want to praise you with my lips
Bathe you with my tongue
Make you see the stars again
Like you did when you were young

I want to do things to you now
Give love I never gave before
Fulfilling your wildest dreams
Until you ask only me for more

Con't

Ubiquitous

I want to show you certain pleasures
No one will ever know but us
Then long after your busy day starts
The love will be Ubiquitous

LOOKING

Living out my life
With little or no regret
Looking for something better
But I haven't found it yet

Or at least that's what I thought
From everything I had seen
Thinking that the grass on the other side
Was a different shade of green

While already inside my pastures
Were fields of pure delight
Unable to see the forest for the trees
I could not tell day from night

Con't

Looking

And then one day it struck me
Like a brick falling from the sky
Everything begins and ends with you
Because You are the reason why

You can search for miles and miles around
Until there's no place left to go
What you're looking for is not airborn
But is closer than you know

FAITH

The measuring of Faith
Evolves from the tried and proven true
While your actions and ability
All play a part in that too

Prayer without works
We all know is dead
Actions always speak louder
Than anything anyone has said

To have faith in another
You must first know them well
Allowing the benefit of the doubt
You still cannot tell

Con't

Faith

Clearly their actions
Make your reactions easy to reply
But not when your response
Is feeding a lie

You always end up
The way you start out
While nurturing a falsehood
In the end leaves you in doubt

In conclusion to this verbal joust
There is only one thing left to say
Life at its longest is way too short
Live your best and all in your own way

A MATTER OF TIME

The charming Gardner
Who makes my heart blossom
Weaving dreams of silk
And the softest of cotton

This horticulturist of my spirit
I found quite by surprise
Never realizing before
Right in front of my eyes

I was once in a dark place
Not knowing where to go
Stumbling through life
Going where I never know

Con't.

A Matter Of Time

Once someone said "Life is hard"
I thought: "Compared to what"
We create our own standards to live by
So what is there left to discuss

Just about everything in life
Begins in the mind
Only becoming a reality
In a matter of time

"That the art of Life
Is creative imaginative and individual
Does not mean
It cannot be taught and learned
Or that Individuals cannot improve
Their mastery of it
This art requires continuous
Creative effort
Drawing on one's character
Circumstances experience and ideals"

Printed in the United States
by Baker & Taylor Publisher Services